ISBN: 9798673590997
Imprint: Independently published

Cover design by: Colin Difilippo
colindifilippo68@gmail.com
Instagram: @colinjames.gfx

Pamela R. Steele
PO Box 25383 Wapiti Center, Grande Prairie, AB, T8W 0G2

Email: pamela@MadeOnPurpose.ca
Web: www.madeonpurpose.ca
www.facebook.com/MadeOnPurpose
Insta: @made_onpurpose

In Times Of Isolation

Meditations For The Lonely Heart

Pamela R. Steele

ACKNOWLEDGMENTS

A special thank-you goes out to all those who contributed to this book by sharing their own stories with me. Also, thank-you to my husband and children, who graciously stepped in and picked up the slack around the house while I buried myself in my writing. And most of all, I am thankful to God who has shown me his heart as my Father and my faithful friend. Thank-you, Father, that you saw me in my darkest and loneliest places and still called me yours - letting me feel your closeness and your love. Without it, I wouldn't be here today.

CONTENTS

INTRODUCTION
I Was Never Alone

When you're going through hard times, it is incredibly easy to fall into the trap of believing that you are alone in it. It is easy to tell yourself that no-one would understand what you are going through.

Isolation is a prison you can put yourself into all on your own by how you perceive your situation. Sometimes, in a strange way, telling yourself that you are alone in your misery can lend to you some sort of quasi comfort. It plays into a victim mentality, even if that is not your intention or desire. It justifies how you feel and the way you deal with how you feel.

To believe that your situation is so unique that there is no one who could relate or understand it, puts you in a very vulnerable and precarious situation mentally, emotionally and perhaps at times even physically.

No matter how alone you feel in your situation, you are not alone. This is so hard to truly embrace when your heart is hurting so.

There were long periods of time, during the years following my divorce, that I felt very much alone. In a physical sense, I was alone as I lacked the support that comes from having close connection and community with others. I lived several years in a city far enough away from my family, that visits and physical help with practical things such as babysitting, or just a real hug when I needed, was not accessible. In an emotional sense, my heart felt very much isolated. The lack of community in my life meant that the relationships I did have were more surface relationships, and not deep heart connections. And, in a way, I was afraid to let anyone truly see the amount of pain I was carrying in my heart, for fear of scaring people away from me. I felt as if there was no place truly safe enough for me to bare my heart and find comfort - except in my private prayers with my Father, God. I knew he understood me. Yet, I questioned at times if he actually cared.

I'm so thankful that God is not afraid of our humanness. I'm so thankful that Father God let me crawl onto his lap and cry my tears without judging me or telling me to shape up while comparing my situation to the many others in the world whose lives were immensely more difficult than mine. No, he never judged me. He only loved me. He loved me in my brokenness and through my brokenness. Although I was in a self-preservation mode and had built a protective wall around my heart, I knew that with Him was the one place that I could lay it all bare before him.

The Bible tells us that Jesus was not unacquainted with grief. In Isaiah 53:3 it tells us that we was despised and rejected and that we in essence hid our faces from him. Talk about loneliness! The very ones he came to save, the very ones he came to give his life for, rejected him. Jesus knows the pain of your loneliness. He knows the pain of rejection.

In Hebrews we read that he understands our weaknesses and temptations. He understands your humanity, because as a man he was tempted in every way, yet, he conquered over sin.

> *"He is despised and rejected by men,*
> *A Man of sorrows and*
> *acquainted with grief.*
> *And we hid, as it were, our faces from Him;*
> *He was despised, and we did not esteem Him."*

That you are completely alone is one of the enemies most effective lies. If he can get you to believe that, then you are much more susceptible to his attacks. If you are truly all alone, you do not cry out for help - for who would you call to? If you are truly alone, then fear becomes an easy companion. For who will stand with you against the evil one?

"I am alone!" you say.

"I have no one."

"Those who are dear to me are no more."

"I have never been wanted."

"No one knows and no one cares about what I am going through."

"I deal with life my way - alone."

"At least no one can hurt me this way."

Have these thoughts ever been yours? How about the forced isolation that comes from circumstances outside of your control?

When the Holy Spirit put it on my heart to write this meditation for lonely hearts, my first thought was, "Oh ya. I've got this - easy. I have LIVED loneliness and survived. I can totally write a quick meditation on the topic." Little did I know how hard it would actually be. You see, I had indeed walked a lonely path for many years. I felt, however, that the realization

I had had through those years of the nearness of Jesus to me and his friendship with me, was all I needed. Yet, as I sat down to write what I felt should just flow out of me, I found myself coming up dry. I was frustrated. I put the idea away for awhile and spent time taking it to God in prayer. My conversation with God was more of a, "Why can't I get this thing rolling? What's the hold up? Please Father, renew in me a revelation of your closeness to me." And then in frustration I waited.

Opportune times to write kept being buried in the hustle of life and parenting. I began to think that perhaps this meditation for lonely hearts may not be getting written any time soon. Then, quietly, almost unnoticeably the Holy Spirit spoke to me and said that He wanted to do a greater healing in my own heart, and show me again how He was with me every step of the way. I was never alone.

I can say unequivocally, that were it not for the nearness of God to me - even in times where I wanted him to just let me go - I would not be where I am today. In fact, I may not even have come through the most difficult years at all. This is not fatalistic talking, or the victim mindset taking a stand. Rather, it comes from a heart that has walked a truly isolating and lonely road for many years and recognizes God's faithfulness and nearness through it all.

Many of you have been or are now, in a lonely situation. Many are in isolating situations - some outside of your control. You may be in a physically isolating situation, where the contact and connection you've had with the meaningful people in your life just simply cannot happen. Or, you may be dealing with the loneliness that comes from being isolated emotionally. Perhaps, due to life experiences, you have built a protective wall around your heart. You may be around a lot of people, and have a lot of friends, but your heart is never shared. You long for a deeper and more meaningful connection with others, but your heart remains in its safe yet painful prison. I am here to tell you that even when you are alone, you are NEVER alone.

There is one who is not bound by isolation and quarantine laws! There is one who transcends time and distance. There is one who breaks down every isolating wall we build around our hearts. There is one who promises to never leave you. There is one who will stick closer to you than your own family. His name - Jesus. Have you met him?

As you make you way through these short stories and meditations, let Jesus introduce himself to you. He longs to show you his love. He wants to hold you and heal your heart. He wants to restore life and hope to you. Will you let him? If you are ready to let the Healer of Hearts come and heal yours, pray this prayer with me.

"Jesus, I am tired of being and feeling so alone. Will you help me now? Thank you that your love for me is greater than any wrong I have done. I thank you that you paid the price for all my sin when you gave your life on the cross and you made a way for me to be your friend. Please come into my life. I accept your love for me. Amen"

In Times of Isolation

When I Am Alone
The Loneliness of Abuse

Hand on the window, forehead leaning against the cold hard glass - my eyes blankly staring through the window to the empty parking lot on the other side. This home had become my prison. I felt there was no escape. The loneliness and isolation I now lived in was inescapable. Unable to discern if the rain on the window or my own tears were blurring my vision, I stood motionless - staring into the nothingness.

My expanding belly pushed against the wall as I stood there. Time seemed to stand still. Quietly, I reached down with my other hand and held my stomach as if to protect the little one growing in me. Or, perhaps it was attempt to draw some comfort from feeling this life inside me. The sound of my husbands deep breathing brought me out of my trance like state, and I realized that I needed to leave the room or risk waking him with my movement and tears.

How had life come to this? How had I become so unloveable to him? How was it that I was now growing our third child inside of me, and still felt so disdained by him? Obviously, I must be missing something. I needed to do better. But, what do I need to do better?

The cycle is unstoppable. He ignores my very existence with incredible discipline - for weeks at a time. If I do get him to raise his eyes to mine his jaw twitches with angry tension and his eyes glare at me. Why he's angry at me I don't know because he won't say a single word. So, to work I go - mow the lawn before he gets home, fold his shirts all the"right"way and put them away, make all his lunches with extra detail and care, make sure that nothing within my power puts a drain on him. Then, without warning, he will "forgive" me my unknown wrong and I am once again worthy of his attention.

As my mind tried desperately to find answers, I quietly slipped on my sweater and shoes and headed out into the dark and the rain. It was incredibly cold and wet, but somehow the cold rain running down my face and soaking my clothes seemed comforting. It was as if I wasn't crying alone anymore.

I walked and walked - one block and then another. Finally, I came to a very busy intersection and just across from it was a church. Crossing the road I walked up to the church. It stood like a big, dark shadow in the night. Over the entryway of the church there was an alcove - a sheltered area. Walking up to the doors, I tucked myself neatly into a corner beside the doors and under that alcove. There I sat out of the rain, but on the inside my heart was still crying. I had so many questions, and none of the answers I could come up seemed to justify my situation.

As I sat there in the dark, wet and cold, watching the traffic come and go through the intersection, my heart cried out to God.
"God, I don't know what to do."
"Please, help me."

In that moment I felt the nearness of God. It was as if he had come and sat down right beside me. It was as if I could lean my head over and feel his shoulder against my cheek. I stayed there for what seemed like hours - breathing, crying, and resting - resting in the peace that only God can give.

Pulling my front heavy frame up from the cold pavement while stabilizing myself with one hand on the brick wall of the church, I took a deep breath in and let it out in loud sigh. Then looking up across the intersection, towards home, I started my rainy trek back - knowing that whatever lay ahead, I wasn't alone. That no matter how alone I felt, God was always and would always be there.

The loneliness that an abusive partnership creates is like no other. Being married to an abusive person, especially for a mother, can feel like an inescapable prison.

If you were to leave, then how do you care for your children? Where do you go? Will anyone help you?

Sadly, often in the case of emotional and psychological abuse, the outside world will not believe you. You married such a wonderful person after all. Unless they have lived with your abuser, they will likely never know the truth of what life behind the closed doors of your home is truly like. You are alone in your pain, and the lack of belief and support from those you have contact with only lends to the confusion and loneliness that you seem to live in.

There is help for the abused soul. Jesus is there with you. He holds you and cries with you. He knows and feels your pain. In your darkest hour, he's with you. You may not be able to see a way out right now, but, there is help for you! Call out to Jesus for help. He will answer you.

"Rescue me, Lord, for you're my only hero.
Sorrows fill my heart
as I feel helpless, mistreated—
I'm all alone and in misery!
Come closer to me now,
Lord, for I need your mercy.
Turn to me, for my problems
seem to be going from bad to worse.
Only you can free me
from all these troubles!"
Psalm 25:15-17 TPT

"Father, I thank you that even when I am alone, you are close to me. I thank you that your mercy and grace are always available to me. Father, please strengthen my heart. Give me the courage and strength to face each day. I thank you that you promise to give me wisdom when I ask, so I'm asking you for wisdom and understanding to know what to do. Thank-you that even when I don't feel you, you're here with me - that you never leave me alone and I do not need to be afraid. Help me now to carry on in your grace and in your love. Help me now to take hold of courage and to wisely make decisions. I give my life and this situation completely over to you. Thank-you for your love and your power in my life. In Jesus' name, Amen."

Not Quite Good Enough
The Loneliness of Shame

How did it come to this? He felt so empty and numb. The stinging pain of rejection seemed almost a comfort - a type of punishment for all the mistakes and shortcomings he knew he had. In a twisted sense, it almost made him feel like he was doing something noble - paying for his sins. The pain felt good in a way. Like pouring peroxide on an open wound it seemed to sting unbearably for awhile, before turning into a dull numbness.

The lack of sensation in his emotions was a welcomed result. In that moment, Depression and Shame joined arms together with Self-loathing and they huddled around him like a dark and dysfunctional group of new companions. The spark of life and creativity that once burned in his eyes, now burned out and was replaced with a dark and empty stare.

Staring at his feet in the old shag carpet of his new accommodations, he didn't feel the draft sneaking in between the pains of the leaky basement window. And if he did, he didn't care. He deserved to suffer anyway. Lifting his eyes he stared at that cold dark window blankly - his mind replaying the events of his life that had led to this moment.

When he met her he was smitten. But even more wonderful than that, it seemed that she also shared the same sentiment towards him. She was beautiful, exotic, adventurous … To think that he could be the object of her attention and affections nearly took his breath away.

His mind started to wander and he started replaying their adventures together in his mind. They played as if on a large movie screen in his mind. His eyes were open, but to anyone looking at him, they were completely unresponsive to the outside world. No, he was gone now, in another place - reliving his past from a spectators view.

His movie continued to roll as he watched himself on that screen, the main character of the show. The lighting flickered and the ticking of an old fashion screen projector played in his mind as if to properly fill in the atmosphere for this debut.

Suddenly the scene changed and he was lying in bed. Rolling over in the night he reached over but felt nothing. Searching around the bed in the dark with his hand and feeling the emptiness beside him, his stomach lurched and his heart sank. He was almost afraid to open his eyes as if keeping them closed would make it all not real. Shakily he reached over and turned on his bedside lamp. Swallowing hard, he turned slowly and cautiously to view the far side of the bed. Empty. In fact, it was still perfectly made. She hadn't come home. Again.

His stomach churned and he felt dizzy. He was shaking with anger and yet, somehow, he didn't feel he had a right to demand she come clean. You see, he had issues of his own. He knew it. Did she? He didn't know for sure. Maybe she did. At any rate, his shame seemed to trump any perceived right to demand or even expect faithfulness and openness from her.

The scene faded as the movie reel ran out and the lights dimmed on the scene of that tortured man, sitting on the side of the bed slumped forward with his face in his hands. End scene.

The next scenes came in a garbled mess of pictures and scenes. It was a kaleidoscope of images and moving clips swirling on the screen. The volume of each scene would individually rise louder than the others, and the scene would come into focus momentarily to allow for specific script and dialogue to be seen and heard above the rest, before fading back into the spinning collage.

There he was as a boy, trying to get his older brother to acknowledge him. *"Get out of here, stupid"* his brother smirked and pushed him to the ground. Suddenly he's standing in the early morning light looking at a video on the kitchen table. The fleshy images blurred out on the movie case, and the letters "XXX" clearly visible on the title. Something stirred in his belly. It was awful and intoxicating all at the same time. Confusion and shame, already showing themselves on his precious young face.

The rest of the scenes came so quickly you could easily miss them. It was as if someone had hit fast forward. A quick blur of a guy who was supposed to be a friend, but abused him. Another scene where he was making his whole class laugh with his skilled wit, while his teacher scowled from the front of the room.

Suddenly, the movie stopped and then backed up slightly before beginning to play again at regular speed. There he was. The strong silhouette of a musician viewed from back stage looking forward. His long hair swaying and swinging as he made his guitar squeal and shriek. His fingers were like lightening up and down the frets. The ladies in the crowd screamed with delight as if in a competition to get his attention. He basked in it. This is where he belonged he thought to himself. Right there … in that moment … perfect. He was a rock star. The camera view floated around the back of him to one side slowly backing away and coming to the front of the stage and settling backwards into the crowd. The view coming back into focus with this guitar god standing centre screen.

The song ended with a raucous, squealing guitar note bending and pitching through the amplifier, the drummer crashing symbols wildly until the lead singer lifted his arm pausing in mid air … then the raised hand clenched into a fist while his arm forcefully flung out to the side stopping suddenly as if hitting a brick wall. Every instrument was silenced into finality in satisfying unison. End scene.

The next scene was eerily similar to the scene of his current reality. The band had kicked him out and brought in a replacement. There he found himself - sitting alone in his car. Staring. Just staring at the steering wheel in disbelief. The shock and rejection stinging bitterly. His eyes blood shot from too much to drink the night before and his clothes wrinkled and disheveled from wearing them all night. He was angry, but anger seemed unpalatable as a long term companion, so instead he asked anger and rejection to please wear the masks called "victim" and "self-pity". That would be easier to live with. "After all, it's their fault for not treating me fairly," he justified, the pain of his rejection now eased by the new masks of his companions.
End scene.

Again the screen became a blur of scenes on fast forward. There was the scene were he gave his life to God in high school, the days that he worked in church ministry, then meeting his wife and blurs of their courtship. The scenes came faster and faster until the tape ran off the reel - with a bright light flickering on the empty screen - the fast ticking of the projector was all that could be heard.

The room now seemed eerily empty. The emptiness grew in intensity and he felt his discomfort growing rapidly. His breathing became quick and shallow and his skin felt clammy with a cold sweat as ugly Loneliness and Self-hatred started to fill the room and seemingly take all the life oxygen with them. Eyes wide he grasped at the chair's armrests gasping for air, leaning back in his chair as if trying to escape the demons of Loneliness and Self-hatred that were now nose to nose with him, their weight pushing the air from his chest. Squirming and writhing to move his eyes from their penetrating gaze he managed to wheeze in desperation, *"Je ... Jesus."* Suddenly the evil eyes of loneliness and self-hatred darted and then narrowed and the shrieked in terror and rage, *"NO! Don't say that name!"* Again they started to press up onto his chest and wrap their boney arms around him to squeeze out any remaining sense of love and purpose out of him ... but he caught his breath and this time yelled *"JESUS!"*

As if struck by lightening, loneliness and self-hatred flew backwards crashing into the set with so much force that the entire stage of his life crumbled in on top of them - the noise of the falling chunks of wood and plaster board competing with the screams from the demons who had just lost their power. Then out of the the settling dust a light began to shine. It got brighter and brighter until he could no longer look directly at it. Out of the light he saw a man walking towards him. His eyes so kind and full of love, he couldn't bear to look upon his face. Yet, he had to. That face - it drew him in. Those eyes - they looked right through him. They saw all of him. There was no way to hide anything from that gaze. Yet, there was no anger or judgment in them. Instead, there was love - complete and unhindered - towards him. He started to tremble as this man closed the distance between them. He did not tremble in fear, but rather in the unexplainable power of love. Love that saw every wrong - every horrible shameful thing - yet did not waiver.

Those eyes of love now right in front of him as the man's hand reached out and raised up his chin until their eyes met. Staring into those eyes, no words would come. Tears began to flow down his cheeks, and in surprise tears started to flow from the eyes of this man. It was as if this man could feel everything that he felt. He wanted to ask, *"Why?" "How?"*, but the words wouldn't come. Finally he heard his lips utter his name, *"Jesus."*

Taking his hand, Jesus pulled him to his feet. Then, placing a hand on his shoulder, Jesus looked into his eyes he said,

"Come. Let's watch this story again. But this time, your eyes will be able to see me as well. You'll see as my heart breaks with yours. You'll see the times you carried pain that wasn't meant for you, and how I longed to carry it instead. You'll see how in your darkest times, the times you want to hide from everyone else, you'll see me there waiting for you. I was never far from you, my son. I've always been as close as the mention of my name.

Today you called to me, and I answered. Today, you called me in your desperateness, and loneliness, and I came to you. In your

weakest hour I will show you my strength. In your most wretched shame, I will show you my forgiveness and my grace. In your brokenness, I will show you restoration. You, my child, are mine. You will never be alone."

Shame causes us to build walls around our hearts. Not only that, but it can cause us to keep those around us at arms length for fear they may see the "real you", and be as disappointed in you as you are. So, in an effort of self-preservation, you build a carefully crafted wall around yourself. For some this wall can also manifest itself physically. For example; often times men and/or women who have suffered sexual abuse as children and youth, will take to food for comfort. In many cases, they are subconsciously building a layer of protection around themselves by over-eating, so that no one would be able to get close enough to hurt them again.

The problem is, that no matter how many layers are built around their hearts or their physical bodies, their emotional pain is not finding healing. Their pain is being hidden and protected. It stays there, forever dictating a life of shame for its carrier.

God wants to heal you and free you from any shame that you are weighed down under. The Bible tells us that ANYONE who calls on him will be saved. God is not a respecter of persons - meaning, he doesn't look at someone over there and admire them because they're so good, and then look back at you and despise you because you are so bad. No! He sees all through the same lens should you accept his forgiveness.

There is no deed so wrong or so praise-worthy that it could make God love you any less or any more. His love for you is free, because his son, Jesus, already paid the price for every wrong you could ever, and will ever do. Don't spend another minute living under shame and self-loathing. Accept Jesus' love for you. He longs to be close to you.

Open your heart now. You can trust him, for he is gentle and kind with your heart. Let him come now and heal those broken pieces. You can experience his love for you today.

"Father, I feel so ashamed of who I am and the things I've done. I know that you know my thoughts, but I'm even ashamed of those! Father, please forgive me all my failings and let me know your love - your full and complete love for me. Help me now to live with my head held high - knowing that I am loved by you. Help me now to see myself the way you see me - as precious, loved and treasured. I pray this in Jesus' name. Amen"

"In the very thought of Jesus
His presence can be found
He's as close as the mention of His name
There is never any distance
between my Lord and me
He's as close as the mention of His name
In my hour of struggle
so many times I've found
He's as close as the mention of His name
Just to breathe the name of Jesus
can turn everything around
He's as close as the mention of His name."

~Gordon Jensen 1978 ~

In The Desert
When God Isn't Enough

Excitement and a feeling of adventure filled the air. The sense that great things were ahead filled the woman's heart with anticipation for what was to come - both the known and the unknown. Today, she was leaving her homeland of Canada and traveling to Texas with her husband and baby to start a new life together. It felt as though the world was her oyster.

Being one who thrived on connection with other people and making new friends, she was in her element with all the new people to start relationships with. Everything seemed to be going so well.

Over the years the woman's friend group grew and so did her influence. She began writing and sharing her heart on a new blog. She was well connected in her church and had a solid core of close friends. There was never a lack of other moms to call to arrange a playdate and have coffee with. She and her husband were well connected and involved in their local church. Although away from her Canadian family, loneliness was not something that really entered her emotional radar. She was happy here - in her element.

As time went on, change was in the wind. Feeling the pull to move to another city, the woman, her husband and now two young children, moved 4 hours away to again start a new adventure together. Leaving behind her friends and the community that she had been welcomed into, and grown in for the last 8 years, felt excruciatingly painful - as though a piece of her heart was being torn from her, leaving an open wound.

Upon settling in their new home city, they began to look for a church community and started the work of building connections with new people and places. Yet, there was a deep loneliness settling into the woman's soul. After a much needed getaway with her husband, she felt a renewed motivation to live life again - to continue to build connections with people and to re-ignite the passions she had inside of her. But, close on the heals of their return home, the world went into isolation due to the 2020 Corona virus scare.

Suddenly, meeting with other moms wasn't an option anymore. Attending church and connecting with the people there was taken away. She felt very much alone. The pain of loneliness was so pervasive and heavy, that at times just getting through the tasks of the day took all her motivation. Then, a depression and sadness would just stay with her. She cried more than she can remember crying and her heart ached. This new city full of promise and adventure felt more like a desert than a promised land.

In these times she chooses to find strength to face another day by spending time with Jesus. In her heart she hears God asking, *"Am I enough?"*. Sometimes, in honesty, she says, *"No, it doesn't feel like you're enough"* and the tears come. But, she feels God with her in spite of her pain. He listens to her pour out her heart and even sits and cries with her and holds her in His arms, because He knows her pain.

Have you had times when you feel like God isn't enough? When it feels as though everything and everyone has been taken from you, and all that's left is Him - is He enough? It's a beautiful thing that God never expects us to give him the right answers. He isn't afraid of our pain. In fact, he is well acquainted with the pain of loneliness. And when you feel like God isn't enough, He doesn't get offended and turn his back on you. He'll always be there. Through the good days and the bad, through the heart ache and the pain, he's there.

Losing community with others is painful! God by his very nature is community - Father, Son and Holy Spirit. We were created to be in community with God and with others. These times of increased isolation from others pose a very difficult emotional landscape for many. No one was meant to do life alone - no one. If you're finding yourself struggling with the heaviness and pain of loneliness in these isolating times, know that you are not alone.

All over the world people are struggling with this very same thing. Don't neglect spending time with God in prayer. Even when it doesn't feel like it, He's there and will give you strength and comfort for another day. And in your times of prayer don't fear being honest about your feelings with God. Nothing you can say, nothing that you can feel, nothing that you can do, can scare him away from you.

Even the Psalmist, David, at times felt like God wasn't with him. His honest and heart wrenching writings now help us walk through our own feelings of pain and abandonment, and know that God is and always will be faithful.

"I'm Hurting, Lord—
Will You Forget Me Forever?
How Much Longer, Lord?
Will You Look the Other Way
When I'm in Need?
How Much Longer Must I Cling
To This Constant Grief?
I've Endured This Shaking of my Soul.
So How Much Longer
Will my Enemy Have the Upper Hand?
It's Been Long Enough!
Take a Good Look at Me, God,
And Answer Me!
Breathe Your Life Into my Spirit.
Bring Light to my Eyes
In This Pitch-Black Darkness
Or I Will Sleep the Sleep of Death.

Don't Let my Enemy Proclaim,
"I've Prevailed Over Him."
For All my Adversaries
Will Celebrate When I Fall.
Lord, I Have Always Trusted in Your
Kindness, So Answer Me.
I Will Yet Celebrate With Passion and Joy
When Your Salvation Lifts Me Up.
I Will Sing my Song of Joy to You,
The Most High,
For in all of This You Have
Strengthened my Soul.
My Enemies Say That I Have no Saviour,
but I Know That I Have One in You!"

Psalms 13 TPT

"Father, I have been struggling with loneliness. I miss my friends and feel like I have a gaping, raw hole in my soul right now. Thank-you that I can come to you when I feel less than perfect. Help me to know and understand your love for me. Help me to draw strength from you each and every day. Thank-you for bringing your peace and comfort to my heart as I fix my focus on you. In Jesus' name I pray. Amen."

Where Do I Fit

I Know They Don't Like Me

There were kids everywhere. Everywhere he turned his view was blocked by the crowds gathering and pushing trying to get to the doors of the school to see if their names were on that entrance or perhaps a different one. Shouts of excitement and groups of kids running towards each other and hugging and excitedly talking over each other about their exploits over the summer. Kids and parents alike pushed past him bumping him while they past - seemingly oblivious to the small boy standing there. Backing up he pressed his back into his mother's legs and stared at the ground to try and block out all the craziness and noise that was going on around him.

It was the first day of school. Not only that, but it was the first day at another new school, and its introduction felt no less intimidating and overwhelming than any of the others had. This was in fact his third school in just 3 years. Thinking back over the last couple years of school gave the boy no comfort for what lay ahead of him now. All the emotions from the last school year were slamming him with the intensity of a tidal wave and he felt his stomach tightening and his breathing quickened. He wanted to cry and his eyes burned. Yet, even just the fact that tears were threatening to spill onto his cheeks filled him with rage that those tears would dare betray him and draw attention to him there now.

Drowning in the noise of the memories and emotions of the past, he hears his mother as if through a din of echoing noise and blurry light, *"Matthew, Matthew, it's time to go in. They're opening the doors honey."* Without really hearing her, his small fingers instinctively tightened their grip around hers and he wondered if she knew how badly he just wanted to stay with her.

Suddenly he found himself moving forward towards the door. How? He didn't know. It was as though a numbness had settled over him and he was being dragged by his feet, one in front of the other - those betraying rebellious feet - taking him where he did not want to go.

The hallways inside were a buzz of activity and kids - and parents trying to locate their children's names on lists pinned to doors. There were children clinging to parents' legs or performing silly goofy antics for whoever might be paying attention, even though there was no space to do so. Teachers were calling out instructions and directing parents like traffic cops. It all echoed in his ears and he turned his eyes to the floor in an effort to try and calm the swirling thoughts in his mind.

Finally, they reached the gymnasium and Matthew's mother found them a clear space of floor where they could stand and wait for the opening address from the principal. An occasional parent or teacher would come and stand nearby and the boy could hear his mother engaging in pleasant conversation and introductions, but he wanted none of it. *"Please don't mention me. Please don't mention me,"* he was pleading in his mind. *"Don't make me talk to them."*

The principal's welcome came and went in a blur. Matthew felt as though he didn't hear a word, because he was trying to calm the panic on the inside as he felt that the time for his mother to leave was coming much too rapidly. He felt as if he was going to explode and the tears became ever more threatening, but in anger he fought them into submission.

Then as if he was in a court of law, and the time to announce his sentencing had come, his mother knelt down in front of him and said, *"Honey, it's time! You get to meet your new teacher and make some new friends."* For the first time since they left the house that morning, the boy lifted his eyes to hers. She seemed excited for him, but was that a flicker of sadness? Could she see how much he was hurting and afraid? Maybe there was still hope. In one last desperate attempt to free himself from this horrible place, he threw his arms around his mother and pressed his face into her stomach and the tears started to come. *"Mommy, please don't leave me! Please don't leave me here. I want to stay with you, Mommy!"* His mother held him close and kept speaking words that he was sure were an attempt to help him feel better, but they didn't. All they did was confirm that there was no escaping this. He was going to be separated from his Mother again and forced to face the unfriendliness and loneliness he had become familiar with in school settings.

You see, he had always felt like an outsider when he was around other kids. His life was different from the other kids', or so he thought. He had a hard time connecting and having fun, and this caused the other kids to react to him poorly. So, his focus became his school work, not so much friends - because, after all, they didn't like him anyway. No one ever asked him to play, and if he came to join them they would act like he wasn't there. When he joined into the conversation, the annoyance or frustration he seemed to cause was very evident to him. No, it was just easier to sit alone and watch.

Matthew's mother's heart felt like it was being torn to shreds. She couldn't leave him here. She just couldn't. But, she had to. *"God! Help my baby! Help my child! ... God ... help me"* her heart screamed as hot tears threatened to spill. *"Hold it together, woman!"* she scolded herself, *"He needs to see how confident and capable you think he is right. Come on now. Be strong."*

Every fibre of her being wanted to scoop her son up into her arms and take him away with her. *"Just for today would be ok, right?"* she reasoned to herself, her logic and emotions in an all out war with each other. *"No! Your boss won't allow him at your work. And you MUST work. You have to step up now and do what needs to be done to take care of him"* her mind fired back.

Leaving her child standing in that crowd of new classmates, staring at his feet in what looked like utter defeat and sadness, was the final straw. As she rushed to her vehicle to make up for time, the ever threatening tears began to breach their safe guards and spill down her cheeks. She felt defeated, helpless and alone. Sitting in the driver's seat, seat belt fastened, and vehicle running she sat staring down at the phone in her hands as her thumb slid across the screen to unlock it as though she had someone to text or call. Her tears splashing off the screen.

Sliding her thumb across the screen she paused and stared numbly at the smeared screen. Who was she kidding? There was no one to call. Her mind wandered to years earlier when she had left her husband to make a better life for her kids. Life was better, but also harder in some ways. The unpredictability that Matthew and his siblings had to put up with for legal reasons crushed her. Yet, she knew that if she had stayed, things would've been much worse.

"God, I need 10 of me to do this! How can I be there for my children and still work every day? God, bring good from all this for my son. Let him be a shining light for you. Please, hold him when he feels alone and let him feel you with him" she prayed in a whisper, her eyes closed, the tears now drying and making her face feel that awkward half dry-half wet feeling.

"Bvvvvv Bvvvvvvvvv" her phone buzzed and brought her back to the present - a text from the boss. It's time to get rolling. *"Here we go. Another day. Lord, please give me strength."*

When you have traumatic experiences as a child, the trauma and emotion can be carried into adult life. It may present in a subconscious system of beliefs that you operate under. For example, if like Matthew you experienced the loneliness of rejection, you could start to believe that there is something inherently wrong and unlovable about you. And, without even intending to, you may pull away from people even though you're suffering deep loneliness and desire connection. You may sabotage a promising relationship or friendship so that the other person won't have the chance to reject you and hurt you that way. You may keep everyone at arms length and put on a facade of being incredibly friendly or popular. But, at the end of the day, you may still feel very alone.

You could be like this child's mother - navigating a difficult road as a single parent where every decision, even for the greater good, carries significant sacrifice and consequence. Where it feels as though you'll never be enough to protect your child from the pain of loneliness and the brokenness he or she is experiencing. You may feel as though you are all alone. Who sees you in those moments when your heart is breaking and you would do anything to ease the pain of your child ... but you actually can't? Who sees the hours you work and the tears you cry behind closed doors? Who sees the pain you carry?

The answer may seem trite, and overly simple, but it is the answer none the less. And it is in no way trite or simple. The answer is this - God. God sees your broken heart as your child clings to you begging for something you can't provide for him. God sees you doing your best and still feeling like an utter failure. God sees your children and knows your love for them, and he loves them even more.

How is this answer not trite? God - the creator of the universe, the almighty, all powerful God - he looks down and he sees you. And he doesn't just see you, he cries with you. He holds you. He listens to you and he loves you. It's not only your loneliness he sees. He sees your children too, and he cares for them. God promises to fill the gap that you can't fill. He's not only there for you, but he is there for your children too.

Just like the words of the old Sunday school song say:

> *"Jesus loves me this I know,*
>
> *For the Bible tells me so.*
>
> *Little ones to Him belong,*
>
> *They are weak, but*
>
> *He is strong"*

The little ones belong to Him. They are His, and as such, He holds them in his arms and cares for them. The Bible tells us that God will command his angels to watch over them. You can trust Him in this.

"Be careful that you not corrupt one of these little ones. For I can assure you that in heaven each of their angelic guardians have instant access to my heavenly Father."

Matthew 18:10 TPT

"Father, I thank you that you promise to watch over my children. I thank you that you assign them heavenly guardians to protect them and watch over them. Please comfort my children when they are lonely and afraid. I entrust them to you, and I thank you that you love them even more than I ever could. I declare now that the hardships that my children face, will only serve to strengthen them and draw them into a close and loving relationship with you. I thank you that you make my children like strong trees that can withstand the winds of adversity and will provide hope for all those they encounter in their lives. I pray this in Jesus' name. Amen"

The Power of Purpose

Why Knowing You Matter Matters

She stood there - staring at herself in the mirror. Part of her hated the person staring back at her with her face soaked in tears and make-up running everywhere. How come she couldn't just get it together? Looking deep into the face of her reflection, a part of her desperately wanted to help that pathetic person staring back at her too. She felt the pain she saw in those eyes and leaking down that face. She felt the agonizing pain of loneliness that she saw in the dropped shoulders and the exhaustion in the back that slumped lower in a look of defeat.

She hated feeling hopeless, because she was a fighter. Her motto had always been, "If life sucks, make it better!" And in many ways she had.

After six years in an abusive marriage, she made the heart wrenching, but freeing decision to do better for herself and her kids by leaving that marriage. That took courage!

Then for several years she had taken on the legal system to fight for the emotional and physical well-being of her children. That took tenacity!

Then, not having her high school diploma had become a hindrance in her furthering her professional capacity, so while working full time, being her own lawyer, and being a mother, she studied and finally graduated from high school officially. That took determination!

She worked herself off of income support by taking on a number of different jobs including a full time day-home, and then re-entered the workforce where she quickly ranked her way up into one of the top sales positions in her work place. Then, wanting to open more possibilities up for herself and her children, still in the midst of years of legal proceedings, she accepted a new employment opportunity in another city where she could enter the real estate field and work towards her licensing to become a real estate agent.

Through every hardship and emotional battle, she never gave up. She was always moving forwards. Always. Now settled in a new city she had endured a 3 month battle to be able to have her children come to their new home.

So, she traveled every weekend that she could to be with them.

Finally, when they were all settled together in their new city, and in a home that she had been able to purchase, they began their new lives - new schools, new work, new churches, new friends. At the same time, another custody battle was initiated by her ex and she spent her evenings drinking energy shots and doing legal paperwork, only to crash for a couple hours before waking the kids up to start another day.

Even so, in the midst of being her own lawyer, working full time, and being full time mother and emotional support to her children, she completed her real estate training and became a licensed agent in little more than a years time. Then in less than a year she listed her first million dollar home. The Lord was blessing her efforts, and she had a natural ability that brought veterans of the industry to her to ask how she was doing it.

Sitting still and letting life have its way with her was never her style. Yet, the time in this new city had started to take a toll on her emotionally and physically. The legal obligations made building connections with a new church or a new friend group almost impossible to maintain. The battle she had been waging, in an effort to be able to better provide for her children, was starting to slowly kill her. The years of extreme stress physically, mentally and emotionally were starting to win the battle. Every day was a fight. She felt herself starting to crumble.

She held it together for the kids. But in private she often couldn't stop crying. She was literally living on fumes and there was no relief in sight aside from an outright miracle. Would her ex ever stop trying to sabotage her moving forward in life? Would she be battling forever to protect her children? How much longer could she keep going?

Looking up again at the face in the mirror, still blurred from the tears in her own eyes. Her face and neck uncomfortable damp from the onslaught of painful sobs. Looking at that face she so wanted to be able to feel proud of her tenacity and accomplishments. Instead, she saw a weak, tired, lonely, exhausted shell of a woman - desperate for a break in the pressure, a chance to take a breath. There was no break coming. There was no way to predict when or if something truly miraculous would happen any time soon.

No, she had to keep going. But, for the first time in years, she really didn't know if she could. Every other time when things got incredibly hard, she could take some time, connect with loved ones, encourage herself and get back at it. Not this time. Not again. She longed for deep sleep. For rest. But even sleep evaded her now. Her bed mocked her.

She remembered how it felt to nearly die when she had given birth to one of her children. She had hemorrhaged badly and was loosing consciousness. In the distance she could hear the midwife and her husband fussing and yelling trying to keep her connected with them. But they were so distant. She remembered staring at the brick of the fireplace across from where she was laying and feeling a total and oh so comfortable peace settle over her entire body. It felt so peaceful, and she was so tired. Then she thought, *"I just had a baby. I don't want him to grow up without me. He needs his mother."* And in that moment, with a sluggish effort she strained to listen to the midwife calling her name and hear her husbands voice. Their voices slowly became more clear, and she noticed the look of relief on their faces. She was back.

"God!" she cried. "God … if it weren't for my children, I'd be done right now … God, I'd walk in front of the next bus, if it wasn't for them. I can't leave them alone, but I'm so so tired, God. I'm so tired. God, I'm so lonely. Help me. Please help me."

In that moment, she felt a whisper deep inside of her, *"You've got more to live for. You're not done yet." "You are here for a reason. Don't give up."* As the voice finished, her chin dropped to her chest and a fresh wave of tears and sobs shook her body. She fell to the floor and wrapped her arms around her legs and rolled into a ball on the floor. Sobbing, she lied there drawing on the strength that only God could give her. She forced her mind to dwell on the sense of purpose that was re-stirred within her just moments ago. *"God, you have to help me. I can't get through this on my own."*

The days following did not become easier for another few years. In fact, they often got harder and more intense. And if you want to hear now that that was the last time she told God that she didn't want to do it anymore, you are mistaken. There were many more nights that she stood in the bathroom, broken and alone, empty and tired, crying out to God - begging for relief and breakthrough. But, she never quit. Do you know why?

The reason she kept going was not because she was some sort of hero or super woman. No, the reason she kept going was because she knew deep within her, that she had purpose. She knew that there was a reason for her being on this earth. She knew that God had given her purpose when he created her, and somehow, if she could just keep going and not give up, she would be able to realize that in her lifetime.

You see, understanding that you have a purpose, is a powerful weapon when it comes to overcoming hardships in your life. Whether your battle is with loneliness, sickness and pain, emotional difficulties, financial struggles - whatever your battle is, knowing that you have a purpose and something valuable and unique to offer is powerful!

Having a strong sense of purpose gives you the ability to look beyond the now and see your future with hope. Your sense of purpose will also empower you in the now because you will start to see every day and every battle as a piece of the puzzle for the greater purpose.

Let's take a look at purpose for a moment. When I'm talking about purpose, I'm not talking about the world's idea of purpose. There is nothing unique, special or extraordinary about the world's view of purpose. How unique and special does the following statements make you feel, "You can do anything you put your mind to." "Anyone can do anything." That's certainly not a celebration of a beautifully unique you! No, the world's design for purpose is an anti-purpose doctrine.

From the time you start grade school you are taught that human kind is nothing other than an accident - perhaps a fortunate accident - but a fortunate happenstance at best. The theory of evolution devalues your worth. It tells you that you evolved from nothing. You're just another form of animal. How does this instil any sense of unique purpose and design? It can't. It simply can't. Right from the moment you start your formal education, the idea that you are special and unique is being taught out of you.

God's idea of purpose is much different. For example, the scriptures tell us of the personal and loving attention that went into your becoming. In Psalm 139:13-14 the psalmist is in awe of God's attention to detail in forming him in his mother's womb. He says that he was created amazingly and uniquely. God was involved in every part of you becoming you. He created you and stitched you together while you were still in your mother's womb.

The Bible says that we are fearfully and wonderfully made. He knew you before you were born. You are his! He knows the number of hairs on your head. There is no possible way that you were an accident. Yes, the circumstances surrounding your conception may not have been ideal, but God and God alone was responsible for giving you life and creating you - beautiful, unique, amazing you. There are no accidents!

The Bible tells us that God delights in you as a father delights in his children. You are his! He created you unique - there is no one just like you. He put things in you - desires, abilities, talents, and gifts, and when you use them, you are being who he made you to be. When you are being you, it brings joy to God.

Purpose doesn't have to be some obscure, foggy notion of a distant hope for a feeling of satisfaction in life. Don't over complicate it. You don't have to spend months staring into your navel trying to find your true self. In fact, the Bible tells us that we are made in the image of God, so it stands to reason that the more you get to know God, the more you're going to know about yourself. God promises that when we draw near to him, he also draws near to us. No one knows you like God the Father knows you. He created you! He put treasures in you. And he will help you find them.

My husband loves to tell the story of this man and his search of purpose. This man was getting on in years and had chosen to retire. However, he was now faced with the uncertainty of what retirement looked like. What does he do now? He still felt that he had a lot of life to live, but, what was life going to look like now? At church one Sunday, the pastor offered to pray for those who desired, so the man's wife gave him a nudge to go forward. Now his wife figured that since her husband was now retired, he could truly give himself to his God given purpose by getting involved in church ministry of some sort. He should teach or preach, or lead a Bible study group or something along those lines. Reaching the front, the pastor came to pray with him and asked what he wanted prayer for.

The man explained how he'd recently retired, but didn't really know what his purpose was, and as such wasn't sure what to do with his time now that he no longer needed to work. The pastor got a bit of an amused smile and asked the man, *"What do you enjoy doing?"* The old man wasted no time in telling the pastor how much he enjoyed working on and restoring old cars. The pastor smiled and simply said, *"Then go work on old cars."*

The old man's wife was not happy with the pastors advice and felt indignant. However, her husband was beaming. It was as if someone had flicked the "life" switch on, and he had just come alive. So, with some consternation, she stayed quiet to watch the inevitable failure of her husbands endeavour. How could tinkering with old cars in their garage be living his purpose? How in the world would that bring as much benefit as her husband could offer if he was teaching or preaching in the church?

Well, the old man started his "tinkering" in their garage. And as he worked on his cars, with his garage door open, young people would stop in front of their driveway and comment on his cars with interest and curiosity. That old man ended up building relationships with and speaking into the lives of several young men in his community during the years that he tinkered on old cars in their driveway.

You see, purpose does not have to be complicated. God has already put it in you. If you don't know what you enjoy or what you're good at, start with getting to know God. Remember, you are made in his image. You look so much like your Father. And he knows you better and more deeply than you even know yourself. Let him start to show you the treasures he's put in you. And as you start to become who he created you to be, not only are you going to feel more fulfilled and happy in life, but you are bringing such pleasure to God's heart as well.

You Formed my Innermost Being, Shaping my Delicate Inside
And my Intricate Outside,
And Wove Them All Together in my Mother's Womb.
I Thank You, God, for Making Me So Mysteriously Complex!
Everything You Do
Is Marvellously Breathtaking.
It Simply Amazes Me To Think About It!
How Thoroughly You Know Me, Lord!
You Even Formed Every Bone in my Body
When You Created Me in the Secret Place,
Carefully, Skillfully Shaping Me From Nothing to Something.

You Saw Who You Created Me To Be Before I
Became Me!
Before I'd Ever Seen the Light of Day,
The Number of Days You Planned for Me
Were Already Recorded in Your Book.
Every Single Moment
You Are Thinking of Me!
How Precious and Wonderful To Consider
That You Cherish Me Constantly
In Your Every Thought!
O God, Your Desires Toward Me Are More
Than the Grains of Sand on Every Shore!
When I Awake Each Morning,
You're Still With Me.

Psalms 139:13-18 TPT

"Trust in the Lord Completely,

And Do Not Rely on Your Own Opinions.

With All Your Heart

Rely on Him To Guide You,

And He Will Lead You

In Every Decision You Make.

Become Intimate With Him

In Whatever You Do,

And He Will Lead You Wherever You Go."

Proverbs 3:5-6 TPT

"Father, I'm so tired and worn out! I'm sad more often than I'm happy. Father, I sometimes feel like I don't have the strength to do another day like this. But, I thank you that you give me strength when I am weak. I thank you that in my loneliness, you never leave me and you never forsake me. Thank-you that your are faithful - that you love me and created me with purpose. Please comfort the pain in my heart and help me to walk in your strength each and every day. I pray this in Jesus' name. Amen"

It's A Big Exciting World

And Sometimes Lonely

❋ ❋ ❋

He had always been a very capable kid - at least that's the way his memory served him. Today was no different. His stomach churned with excitement and anticipation. Maybe there was a little bit of anxiety in there too, but, his sense of adventure drowned it out.

Life had been quite a whirlwind these last 6 or so months. After his dad was laid off earlier in the summer, their family struggled to keep their heads above water. His dad looked for work every day, while his mother was busy with his baby sister and younger siblings. Not being able to find work, his dad left home to search for work in the North, about 6 hours away.

And find work he did! This was such good news for the family, but it also meant some very big changes were imminent. One of them was the inevitable move to this new city, far from all his friends and familiar things. Right now though, there was more anticipation that this change was going to bring much needed relief to all of them. His ever keen sense of adventure, kept him from pondering too deeply or embracing the grieving emotions of saying goodbye to the friends he'd been with in school for the past five years now. He liked to keep things happy, fun and easy going, and right now, he was excited.

The line of people ahead of him started to shuffle forward as he moved towards the airport security check. He had flown before, but this time was different. This time, he didn't know when he would be coming back. He didn't know how long it would be before he was reunited with his mom and siblings. For all the excitement, there were a lot of unknowns as well. He was going up to join his dad in the north and catch the first day of the second semester of grade nine, in the new school he would be going to. His mom didn't want him to have to start at a new school mid-semester, so she had made the decision to send him up north ahead of the rest of the family. She had to stay behind and deal with selling the house and settle other matters before she could bring his siblings up and join him and his dad for good.

The flight was so much shorter than he had expected it to be. In just over an hour they had already begun their decent. His fresh start had begun. Tomorrow he would be starting at a new school. His dad had secured a place to live that would be home to the family. Everything was new. The streets, the buildings, the landscape, his home - all new and different.

Morning came quickly. He concentrated on calming the thoughts rushing through his mind. *"What's it going to be like?" "I hope my teachers like me." "I wonder if I'll find a new friend group here."* Taking one final glance in the mirror, he fixed his hair and straightened his hoodie. *"Ok. Time to go,"* he said to himself, and off he went.

"The first day went really well," he thought. His teachers all seemed pretty decent, and over the lunch break, a bunch of guys had invited

him to throw the football around for awhile. In fact, the day was awesome. He was elated with the thrill of meeting all his new friends and the excitement and adventure of being so independent.

However, after school and in the the night times, life was a tad more anti-climactic. With his dad working nights at times and his mom and siblings still living in another city, the house was pretty quiet and empty. There was a lot of time to think and to feel. He thought about his friends back "home" and missed them. He really cared about his guys, and now the realization that he may not see some of them for a very long time, or perhaps ever, started to sink in. For the first time that he could remember, he felt lonely. Before, if he was struggling with overwhelming emotions, he would talk it out with his mom. Now, he felt as though he had to handle this all on his own.

After all, his parents had so much on their plates right now. He so wished they could be all together again.

One month passed, and then two. Finally, at the end of his third month, his mother and siblings had been freed to complete the move up north. They could finally all be together again! He knew it would happen. He had never doubted it would happen for a moment. He just didn't know the when or the how. But, he had faith that God was going to bless his family and work out the details that needed His divine intervention - and God did.

When we walk through different challenges in life, and there are so many unknowns and uncertainties, it can be very isolating. This young man had a strong faith in the goodness of God. This helped him to hang on and to have hope. Even the times when he was alone and feeling the sting of loneliness, God was close to him. God is always near.

Parents, when you have to release a child, maybe it's for a visit with an ex partner of yours, or they are going on a trip with their school or youth group, maybe they're spreading their wings and leaving the nest altogether for university or employment, know that God is close to your children. Pray for them. Ask God to bring people across their paths to be good and godly friends to them. Ask God to bring people into their lives who will speak life and encouragement to them. But, mostly pray, that in their dark times and their lonely times, that they learn to call out to the Father and draw their strength from Him. He loves your children even more than you ever could. Isn't that wonderful? You can trust Him with them.

I would have lost heart,
unless I had believed
That I would see the goodness of the Lord
In the land of the living.
Wait on the Lord;
Be of good courage,
And He shall strengthen your heart;
Wait, I say, on the Lord!

Psalms 27:13-14 NKJV

Some friendships don't last for long,
but there is one loving friend
who is joined to your heart
closer than any other!

Proverbs 18:24 TPT

"Father, thank you that in times of uncertainty I can rest in the fact that you are faithful and your Word is truth. Thank-you, Father, that even though things are rough right now, I will see your goodness in my life. And Father, those friends I've had to leave behind, those friends that have walked away, please bless them and watch over them. Please, comfort my heart as I grieve the loss of their connection. And I thank you that you are always with me - you're a friend to me and you are closer to me than any other. Thank-you that you know my heart, and you love me.
I pray this in Jesus' name. Amen."

There Is No "I" In Team

But There's Only Me

The smell of chlorine filled the warm, humid air. Screams of laughter and excitement echoed off the walls as if she was standing in a big empty barrel - the echos filling her ears. It was bright and exciting here. She remembered back to her childhood days, when a trip into town to go to the local swimming pool was a thrill unlike any other. How fun it had been. She remembered how her dad would often come into the pool with them and play games with her and her siblings like having them take turns standing on his shoulders while he'd crouch down in the water, then suddenly launch them upwards like a rocket to go squealing and screaming through the air with pure joy and come down with a huge splash in fits of laughter.

As she glanced around this pool, she noticed the other families there. A woman with a baby that looked like it was only days earlier enjoying the warmth of the womb - the woman's eyes meeting her husband's eyes and sharing a knowing stare together. It was as if their non-verbal connection had no need for words. They were there together, loving each other, and in pure joy and contentment sharing the wonder of this new child … together.

Shifting her gaze around the pool her eyes fell on another family. The mother happily helping a toddler float on her belly, while the father was heartily encouraging their pre-schooler to jump into his arms from the edge of the pool. As the child jumped into his father's arms, both parents erupted into cheers while congratulating the proud little man on his great accomplishment and bravery. Every where she turned it seemed there were families … fathers and mothers together - little huddles of "teams" everywhere.

The shouts of her children broke her out of her trance like state and back to reality. There they were. The most precious and beautiful children she'd ever laid eyes on. Her oldest was yelling at her to watch as he hung off of the climbing wall at the end of the pool. He was going to jump into the pool from there and absolutely needed her to see. She made a concerted effort to watch him and not look away, but at the same time her daughter was hollering to her from the edge of the pool, *"Mum! Mummy! Watch how long I can tread water!!"* with the biggest grin on her beautiful, goggled, little face. Her heart ached with the beauty and innocence of that precious girl staring back at her. SPLASH!!! Her oldest son had just connected with the water after his daring leap from the climbing wall, *"Mum! Mum! Did you see that!!! That was epic! Did you see??"* Not wanting to disappoint she responded, *"Yes! That was incredible!! ... Do it again",* hoping that this time she would actually catch the amazing event.

Just as her oldest started climbing out of the water and up the climbing wall, her youngest son called to her from the lazy river. *"Mum! Mum! Come float with me in here! I'll chase you! ... Please come mummy!"*

"Ok, son, I'll be right there!" she called back, then quickly remembered to look towards the

climbing wall. Oh … and her daughter treading water. *"Wow! Honey! You are doing amazing! I am quite sure I can't tread water for even half as long as you!"*

SPLASH! *"Mum! Mum! Did you see this time? MUM!? That was the most awesomest one yet!! Did you see it?!"*

"Mum! Are you coming! I want to chase you!"

"Mummy, how long was I treading water for? Did you see how I made my legs go out like that? IT helps me stay up better. How long was that? Was it the longest ever?"

Fighting the lump in her throat she tried to answer each of her children and express keen interest in all of their current escapades,

"Oh yes, honey! That was so brave of you! WOW!"

"And you sweet heart, you are the best water treader I've seen yet!"

"Honey! I'm coming! Stay where you are!"

She was trying hard, but she hated coming to the pool for this exact reason. It made her feel so alone, and it was as though there were spotlights shining down from the high ceiling, shining on all these beautiful family units. They were highlighting what she so desired for herself and for her children as if to remind her of what was missing, these spot lights shone down with no compassion or empathy. Her children were the most precious and valuable things in her whole world, but somehow she felt so inadequate. Everything she had and everything she was felt like it just wasn't enough. Her heart ached in loneliness. It was a strange kind of loneliness. Yes, it was her own, but it was as if her own personal lack - her own inability to be everything for her kids - made her lonely for them - for their lack of a complete family. Looking around all she could see were families - fathers and mothers together with their children. Somehow her eyes couldn't see the other single fathers and single mothers there alone.

She felt the deep ache of loneliness like a bruise deep in her chest. The pain pulsed every time she looked into the faces of her precious children. How she wanted to share the wonder and amazement she felt towards them with somebody who was equally in love and in of awe them. She wanted to share those knowing looks with a husband and father as together they notice something amazing or funny and quirky about one of the children. She longed to have someone to join hands with in prayer for her children when they were facing challenges, feeling afraid, writing an exam, lonely for a friend, dealing with bullies at school … all of it. Bottom line - she wanted a partner, a team mate. Yes, a team mate. All she ever wanted was to feel like she was on the same team as her husband. She wanted to know that they were doing this life together - that they were raising these children together. Her heart longed for that feeling of togetherness, the "*you and me and then the world*" kind of connection. Yet, here she was, alone. She was resolute in the mission to never let her heaviness become her children's worry or burden, so she shouldered up under the load and turned the turmoil inward. Swallowing the lump in her throat and quickly blinking back threatening tears, her eyes met the eyes of each of her children and she forced a big grin onto her face and forced her eyes to open wide with a sense of anticipation and excitement for everything they were telling her and experiencing. On the outside she was fully engaged with them. She desperately wanted to be there in the moment with her children, and she wanted them to remember these fun times together. But on the inside, she was waging war with her emotions.

As they played and splashed together, she threw in all the comments and reactions to encourage and recognize her children's enthusiasm for their daring antics, and from the depths of her heart she called out to God. *"Father, you promise to be father to the fatherless. Please, be that for my children. Give me strength to be everything they need me to be. But, God, where I fall short, thank-you for filling in the gaps for me."*

Single parenting is lonely at the best of times. No matter the support you may have through family and friends, at the end of the day it's just you. Just like this lady prayed to God to be a father for her children, you can too. This doesn't mean that you and they will be spared from ever feeling the loneliness and pain that comes from the absence of having a father or mother actively in their lives. But, as a father, God will strengthen their hearts and yours. He will give you grace to go another day, and another, and another. He wants good for you and for your children. He loves them more than anyone. He laughs with amusement when they do funny, quirky things. His heart hurts and is angered when they're mistreated and teased at school. He gets excited about their school band recital and the wrestling tournaments. His eyes fill with tears and he holds them when they're afraid and alone. And, he reaches down and joins hands with you as you come to him, your Father, in prayer for your children. He cries, laughs, rolls his eyes and sighs in awe as you talk together about those children - those precious, beautiful children. After all, they're his children too. He's on your team.

"To the Fatherless He Is a Father.
To the Widow He Is a Champion Friend.
To the Lonely He Makes Them Part of a
Family.

Psalms 68:5 TPT

"Father, I know that I fall short of what my children need. I cannot be both a father and mother to them. Father, my heart aches for them and the loneliness I know they feel for a father. God, I thank you that you promise to be a father to the fatherless. Thank-you that you fill the gaps. Thank-you that you love my children fiercely. Father, I also thank you that you are my champion friend - that you keep me close to your heart and have made it so that I do not have to do this on my own. Thank-you, that you are always, always with me. I pray this in Jesus' name. Amen"

The Power Of A Grateful Heart

Life's Too Short To Worry

* * *

I have been blessed with strong women role models in my family. I find that I think about one or more of them nearly every day now as a woman myself. My grandmother's both paternal and maternal, have been a source of inspiration to me. My paternal grandparents have both entered Glory and are enjoying eternity with Jesus. My last remaining grandparent is my Nana, my maternal grandmother.

Nana is one of the most fascinating people I know. When I was young and had become a newly licensed driver, I used to drive 5 or more hours to pick her up and bring her to stay with me. I tell you what, no one can clean a house top to bottom, organize a kitchen, properly make all the beds and iron the clothes with the speed and efficiency that my Nana could. Then cook? Man, she is the best cook. When my siblings and I were growing up, it was just a little known fact that grandmas are the best cooks in the world.

Nana grew up in England on a farm. On those long drives from her home to mine all those years ago, she would tell me stories of her youth and childhood. She told me of how as a teen she would hurry to get all the farm chores completed, and then she would take off running across the field to the neighbouring farm to visit with my Papa. I was fascinated.

Her life was like a movie - so much drama and adventure. Yet, there was also pain and heartache.

Nana and Papa moved to Canada when my own mother was about 12 years old. They ran a small business and made place for themselves here. Then when I was a young girl, my Papa became sick with cancer. After a long battle, he died. I remember being there in Nana's trailer when he passed away, and hearing the wailing and crying. I couldn't imagine the pain and loneliness that Nana must have been feeling.

Fast forward a few years and Nana started her own battles with cancer. Twice she had surgery for breast cancer, yet I never heard her complain - not once. I saw my Nana carry on with life and do whatever had to be done. I watched my Nana never loose her beautiful confidence and femininity. She still adorned herself with her flashy earrings and bright summery colours. She didn't bemoan her loss from the breast cancer, but rather continued to love herself and enjoy her beauty. For this alone, my Nana is my hero.

Nana never came across as feeling sorry for herself. Instead, she focused on others. Nana always had friends - close friends. To this day, she still holds a Christmas party every December and has all of her friends over to indulge in Christmas baking and a good time. My Nana loves people. She really loves them and values them.

I talked to my Nana recently and asked her if she struggled with loneliness after Papa passed. Her answer was an adamant, *"No!"*. I was a little perplexed, but her perspective was the most amazing thing. You know, she of course grieved the loss of my Papa, her husband, but every day she was thankful. She was thankful for the life she had, for her children and grandchildren. She was thankful for her friends. She was simply thankful.

Even today, well into her eighties, you will be hard pressed to have a conversation with my Nana without hearing about how thankful she is for her family, her life and her friends.

John Maxwell coined the phrase, *"Your attitude determines your altitude."* I can see this so clearly with my Nana. Thankfulness is powerful! You can literally change the way your brain works by teaching yourself to be thankful. I'm not saying that you will never feel sad, or lonely or depressed. Those are all normal emotions. They're real and are experienced by the best of us. But we can change our trajectory in life by learning an attitude of thankfulness.

It can feel very odd and also insincere to start with, but next time you're feeling depressed, sad, lonely or angry, take a moment. Stop moving. Close your eyes and take a deep breath in. Hold it, then slowly release it. Do this again 4 to 5 times. Then, speak out loud 3 things you're thankful for. If you're really feeling down, you may feel like there's nothing at all to be thankful for. How about being thankful that your shoes are comfortable, or that the sun is shining. Or maybe the simple fact that there is life in your body today.

Whatever it is, however simple or silly it feels, start training your brain to default to thankfulness. This will actually change the chemicals your brain releases into your body! Your brain will start to release happiness hormones like serotonin and dopamine instead of stress hormones like cortisol. Over time your cells will actually start to create more receptors for the happy chemicals from your brain than the receptor sites for the stress hormones. This is fascinating, and it means that you can actually cause your body to be more prone to feeling happiness than stress and sadness! You can do this by training yourself the art of thankfulness. And there is no better time than now, to get started.

"Oh, give thanks to the Lord,
for He is good!
For His mercy endures forever."

Psalms 118:1 NKJV

"Thank-you, Father, that you sustain me. Thank-you, that you are good and faithful and true. Thank-you for giving life to my body and peace to my heart and mind. Help me now to live a life of gratitude. Help me to train my heart and my mind to focus on you and your goodness to me. You, oh Lord, are good, and your mercy and love last forever. I pray this now in Jesus' name. Amen."

Count Your Blessings

When Upon Life's Billows
You Are Tempest-Tossed,
When You Are Discouraged,
Thinking all Is Lost,
Count Your Many Blessings,
Name Them One by One,
and It Will Surprise You
What the Lord Has Done.

Are You Ever Burdened
With a Load of Care?
Does the Cross Seem Heavy
You Are Called To Bear?
Count Your Many Blessings
Every Doubt Will Fly,
and You Will Keep Singing
As the Days Go by.

When You Look at Others
With Their Lands and Gold,
Think That Christ Has Promised You
His Wealth Untold;
Count Your Many Blessings
—Money Cannot Buy
Your Reward in Heaven,
Nor Your Home on High.

So, Amid the Conflict
Whether Great or Small,
Do Not Be Discouraged,
God Is Over all;
Count Your Many Blessings,
Angels Will Attend,
Help and Comfort Give You
To Your Journey's End.

~Johnson Oatman Jr., Pub. 1897

Loneliness in Retrospect
From Resentment to Contentment

* * *

The air was crisp and refreshing, and the leaves crunched under her feet with each step. The seasons were definitely changing as the lush green of Summer morphed into the colourful landscape of Autumn. The years seemed to have multiplied quickly on her all of the sudden. She took a deep breath of the cool air into her lungs, then let it out slowly as she paused to take it all in. Happy to be out for some quality time in the fresh air with her owner, Promise yanked at the end of the leash. Eager to keep moving, the excited old dog was impatient with her owner's more relaxed pace. Oddly enough, Promise's pace was slow as she was an old dog herself. Still, it took a concerted effort for the woman to keep up with her furry companion.

Giving in to Promise's urging, she carried forward with her walk. Her mind wandered while watching that big, fluffy, black tail swooshing and bobbing around in front of her. She remembered back to when her husband brought this big black dog home. The poor thing was barely alive. She remembered back to when she had prayed and asked God, if he was willing, to please let her have a black dog. *"Hahahaha!"* she threw her head back in laughter as she remembered that prayer. She wanted a companion, and a black dog would do just fine. She hadn't, however, specified what size of black dog. *"God sure did deliver on this one!"* she thought to herself with a chuckle. Promise was a very, very large black dog.

Stopping again to adjust her weight on her legs and catch her breath, the woman stood staring at Promise as if looking through her into more memories, her mitted hand firmly holding the leash. Promise had come to her at the right time. All of her children were grown and lived far away from her and her husband with their spouses and their own children. Suffice it to say, that spending actual physical time with her sons was a very rare occurrence, even more so since they all married and moved to different locations. She and her husband had also moved to a tiny isolated town, on the West Coast.

Giving in to the tugs on the leash she pressed forward again at a slower pace, deep in thought. Her mind turned from her grown children to when they were still little boys. Life sure was busy then with four young boys. It was a loud and chaotic house at times, but she wouldn't have it any other way. Being a young family, her husband worked a lot, so, she lived for her boys. She loved them. They were her life. Yet, they couldn't be her entire life.

Deep inside she longed for her husband. She so desired his time and attention. But, more than anything, she wanted him to share her faith with her. She wanted to be able to share this part of herself with him. It was her deepest part. The most intimate pieces of her heart. He just wasn't there yet though, so, she poured her emotions into her children, and sought more connection with them to help fill the void she felt.

As Promise continued to lead them down the path, the woman remembered how lonely she had felt for her husband at that time, as light snow flakes began to gently fall - landing on her cheeks before quickly melting away. The path ahead of them suddenly transformed into something magical as gently swirling snowflakes filled the air with confetti that contrasted the bright Fall leaves of orange, red and brown that filled the branches leaning over the path in their regal beauty.

As the snow fell, she remembered that Boxing Day when her husband had agreed to go into work for the day, instead of staying home with the family. Traditionally, Boxing Day had always been just as important as Christmas for her during her childhood years. This was a tradition she so wanted for her young family.

That sense of celebration as they would get together with extended family for the day. But, that wasn't going to happen that year. She remembered standing and staring out their kitchen window and down their driveway to the main gravel road past their acreage. The snow was falling then as well - adding a winter wonderland feel to the whole scene. As she watched the snow falling outside, vehicles were coming down that gravel road, right past their driveway and into the neighbour's yard. She watched as the vehicles pulled up, and happy families jumped out to run and hug her neighbours who were eagerly waiting and waving for their newly arrived company from their front porch.

Stopping again to rest her legs, Promise now happy to plop down on her haunches beside her person, raising her face and nuzzling her wet nose into her palm looking for some encouraging pats and rubs. The woman thought of how she had felt resentment towards her husband because of her loneliness - and perhaps even towards God himself. Remembering the pain of the loneliness in those years, even made her feel anger in that moment. Dropping her chin to her chest she felt those pangs again, she reached over and tussled Promises's floppy ears. Promise thumped her tail on the ground loudly in sheer delight. *"Well, Promise, I sure was lonely then, she said to her companion, but God told me that he feels lonely too, because he longs to spend time with us as well."*

Turning now to walk back towards home, the woman continued to tell Promise how God spoke to her heart and how she had found comfort in how he identified with her pain. In the days and years going forward, she had begun to have a new perspective. When her husband had to work, and she felt isolated and alone being home with her young boys, she started to see herself and her husband as being on a team together. When she stayed home with the boys, her husband was free to do the work that he needed to do, and help those he came in contact with. As she started to see herself as a vital part of the team, she didn't feel so alone anymore. Sure, she still was alone in many ways, but she was learning to view her situation differently. Ultimately, she had learned more than ever, how to draw on God's grace to walk through each day. She felt closer to God than she had in all her life.

As the years went on her heart still ached for her husband to share her faith. Yes, she had learned to be more contented with her own relationship with the Lord, but she so wanted to share this with the man she loved. "*God, I'll move anywhere with him. I'll go anywhere. Just please bring my husband back to you."*

Not long after praying that prayer, they moved to where they now lived - a stunningly beautiful, tiny, isolated mountain town on the coast. It was so peaceful there. The woman paused again for one last rest before closing the distance to the house. This place, was so far away from all her children and their families. Yet, God answered her hearts cry here. It was here that her husband, the man whom she loved, found community in the church. It was here that God got ahold of his heart and made it new and soft towards him. Her deep longing and prayer had been realized.

Moving forward again towards home, she stepped out of the trail head and they were back on the street of their tiny town once again. Their home could be seen just up the block. She smiled as she thought of how her and her husband now hold hands in prayer together. And, when he isn't away working, they walk into church together side-by-side and sing praises together with other believers. Every morning that read devotions together. God heard her prayers.

Yes, of course she still feels loneliness at times for her children and her grandchildren. Her heart can't help but yearn for them. She loves them so. As she thought about these precious ones, a tear snuck down her rosy, chilled cheek. But, in place of the resentment and the pain of loneliness that once plagued her heart with heaviness, she now was filled with thankfulness and contentment. Kicking the snow off of her shoes as she unlocked her front door, she stepped inside. The warm air from the wood stove rushed around them like a warm blanket. Promise made her way to her cozy mat right in front of the wood stove, turned a couple of circles, and then plopped herself down contentedly. While the woman hung up her jacket and placed her mittens on the shelf.

Taking a deep breath in, then straightening up and turning towards the kitchen, she smiled and slowly exhaled. Yes, she was thankful - so very thankful. God had truly been so good to her. And, in her most difficult times, He showed her that he knew, and that he cared. She drew near to him, and he in turn came near to her. No matter what, He was her father and faithful friend, and she was his. She would never be alone again.

Can you relate to this woman? She felt the loneliness that comes with not being able to share her faith with her husband. She wasn't able to share this most intimate part of herself with him. Not only that, but she was home alone a lot, and her desire for meaningful connection and building of family traditions together wasn't being realized. She began to feel resentment and bitterness about her situation, but ultimately she called out to God and he answered her.

Things didn't suddenly turn around for her, but rather, God started to do a work in her own heart. He let her feel his nearness to her, and related to her in her pain. She started to learn how to find contentment in spite of her circumstances, and she began to see her life from a different perspective.

When you call out to God, he will hear you. He will comfort you and walk with you. Your current situation may not immediately change, but your perspective can. As you turn your thoughts and attention to Jesus, He will bring you peace. He will walk through the dark times with you and give you the strength you need to face each day.

Don't Be Obsessed With Money
But Live Content With What You Have,
For You Always Have God's Presence.
For Hasn't He Promised You,
"I Will Never Leave You Alone, Never!
And I Will Not Loosen my Grip on Your Life!"
Hebrews 13:5 TPT

"So We Are Convinced
That Every Detail of our Lives
Is Continually Woven Together
To Fit Into God's Perfect Plan
Of Bringing Good Into our Lives,
For We Are his Lovers
Who Have Been Called To
Fulfill his Designed Purpose."
Romans 8:28 TPT

"Father, some days I feel so lonely. I feel lonely for deep connection with my spouse. I feel lonely for my children and grandchildren. Please help me to find contentment and comfort in you. I thank you that you promise that you will never leave me alone. Thank-you that I can share my heart with you and you are not afraid of how I feel. Thank you, that you are my truest and dearest friend. And that you, Lord, are the lover of my soul. Thank-you, Father that you promise to work good into my life, no matter what my current circumstances look like. Thank-you that you will bring good from the pain that I feel, and that I, in turn, will be able to bring life and hope to others struggling in loneliness.
I pray this now in Jesus' name. Amen"

Longing for Belonging

Here he was again. Years ago he would've been crying and screaming. He may have thrown a fit or tried to break something to try to show how unhappy he was. But that was years ago. Now, he didn't know what he felt really. Sure his heart ached inside of him. But he had learned long ago that his tears meant nothing. In fact, if tears of sadness or fear threatened to spill, it would enrage him and he would let his anger turn off his more vulnerable emotions. *"What's the point in crying?"* He would think to himself. *"It doesn't change anything. It just shows them how weak you are."*

His life seemed like an unstoppable cycle. As he sat in the backseat of the car listening to the hum of the tires over the highway he thought back to when he was just 5 years old. His life now was the fault of that 5 year old boy, or so he told himself. He replayed the events in his mind, staring straight ahead at the back of the seat in front of him. He had been playing in his room most of the day. He had heard some strange people in the house, but that was normal for him. He knew though, to keep his distance. So, that day he closed himself away in his bedroom hoping that no one would come looking for him.

Eventually his hunger got the better of him, and he quietly and carefully ventured out of his room to go and see if anyone had left any food around. Things were unusually quiet as he made his way down the hallway to the kitchen. Their house was small and disheveled. Piles of garbage from take-out dinners were littered throughout. Full ashtrays with half burnt cigarettes were on nearly every surface. The floors were strewn with clothing, and garbage.

As he walked through the kitchen his uneasiness grew. Where was his mother? Why was it so quiet. Passing through the kitchen, he carried his tiny frame into the living room. There she is! There she was - his mother - asleep or so it appeared. But, he was hungry and he needed her. *"Mummy? .... Mummy? ..."* he gently shook her shoulder. She didn't respond or move. *"Mummy?! ... Mummy wake up! . . . MUMMY!!"*

His little heart was beating loudly in his ears and he felt the panic start to take over his body. Tripping over a pile of clothes he grabbed for his mother's cell phone sitting on the end table. Quickly he dialled 911. His mother had taught him to do this, so he knew what to do, *"If I ever fall asleep and you can't wake me up, here's what you have to do ..."* she had made sure he could take care of her in case of an overdose.

"911 What's your emergency?"

Sitting there staring at the back of the car seat in the dark, he wondered what would've happened if he had just hung up the phone right then. Would his mother have woken up? Would they have let him stay with her. Why couldn't he just wake her up instead of calling that number?

From that night until now, he had been placed in home after home after home. Each time he would be ok for a few days. He would even start to hope that the new foster parents would decide that they really liked him, maybe even loved him. Maybe he would get to stay if he was really good. Yet, like a broken record, he seemed to re-live the same scenario over and over and over again.

He would be taken to a new foster family. Sometimes they would seem like really nice people and he'd start to hope he could stay there. Then, something would trigger his anger and his fear and he'd go off - like really go off. He would yell and scream. He would punch the walls and break whatever was in his reach. He didn't really understand why he did it.

Things had been going pretty good this time around. He'd been with a new family for about 2 months now, and although there were some rough patches, he was starting to feel like he might be able to trust them. He was starting to feel himself becoming vulnerable to feeling emotion towards this new family - which he was happy for and hated at the same time. Feeling vulnerable wasn't a safe place to be. Yet, as if a glutton for punishment, he let these feelings of vulnerability start to grow towards his new family. He so desperately wanted them to want him too.

That morning, as he was walking out the door to head to school, he tried to catch the attention of his foster dad. His dad seemed flustered and preoccupied, and gave him a quick, *"Have a good day"* before walking out of the room without looking up from his phone even once to meet the eyes of the boy in front of him.

The boy didn't want to let this bother him as much as it did but, the knife of rejection and loneliness, that felt permanently embedded in his soul, was given a little twist and it caused an almost physical pain in his chest. He quickly and angrily shoved the pain down farther, as he turned to leave for school without another word or attempt to say goodbye to his foster mother.

The rest of his day he couldn't concentrate in class. His mind was flooded with memories - all those memories. Memories of previous foster homes. Memories of his mother. He wasn't sure if he really could remember what she looked like, but he pictured her face in his mind and imagined that she was the most beautiful and loving mother ever. Then he would replay the events of his morning over and over in his mind. His pain grew inside of him the more he re-lived the rejection he had felt that morning - " ... *and right when I was starting to like these guys.*" He thought to himself.

As he walked home he passed an open green space along the path. He walked through this park everyday. Today, though, there was a kid in the field with his dad. The dad would toss a football and shout, *"Go long son! Go long!"* The boy would break out into an all out sprint while turning sideways to look behind him to the coming ball. And like a pro athlete, he jumped about 4 feet in the air, tucked that football under his arm and came tumbling to the ground in a graceful tumble. He watched as the boys father let out a loud, *"Wooohoooo!!!! Way to go, son!"* as he jogged across the field to his son. Reaching down the father grabbed his son's hand to yank him to his feet. Tousling his boy's hair, he laughed and gave his shoulder a playful shove.

Watching this interaction was like the straw that broke the camel's back for him. That short snippet of life that he had just witnessed pushed on all of the sore and hurting parts of his soul. Everything he wanted, he had just witnessed - and now he was angry. He was angry because letting himself be sad wouldn't help anything anyway. He was even angry that he was angry. He didn't like that these feelings made him feel so vulnerable. At least he had football practice tonight. That always seemed to help him release his pent up anger.

By the time he reached home, he felt like a powder keg - like the slightest provocation would put him over the edge. As he came in the front door and into the family room, his foster mom called out, *"Matt, is that you? ... Your coach just called. Practice is cancelled for tonight."*

Without uttering a word, the powder keg in him erupted. Throwing his backpack across the room, he then started yelling and screaming as he rampaged around the living room knocking lamps over and punching the walls.

Next thing he knew, he was being picked up

by the social worker to be placed in another home or with another family. He didn't really know, and he didn't really care. He was in deep despair. Why had he been so awful, scaring his foster mother that way? Perhaps, he wanted to know that when he's ugly and "unloveable", he could actually be loved? That they would actually want to keep him. Maybe he was protecting himself from more rejection, by exiting the situation before anyone could hurt him further. Would he always feel so alone?

The young man was indeed placed with another family. This family had other kids and teens his own age. He hadn't figured out how and where they all fit in yet, but he did know that some were the biological children of the parents here, and, there was at least one other foster child along with one adopted teen. Altogether, there were seven children and teens in this home, including him. He had never been placed with such a large family. Since he had "issues", he was typically placed in homes where he was the only child. He surmised that people were likely afraid that he would harm their other children, so they wouldn't want to take him on. He was a "special" case. So, to now be placed in a home with so many other kids was a new experience.

The other thing that was new and foreign to him was the fact that from the moment he set foot inside the front door of this new home, he could feel how peaceful it was. Once inside, the father of the household rushed around the corner to the front entrance and a huge friendly grin erupted on his rugged and friendly face. The man reached out his arm and grabbed the boy's hand in his giant bear paw and shook it warmly. Not once did his eyes move away from his. *"Welcome! We're so happy you're here with us!"* the man nearly shouted. Then, without any hesitation he gave the boy's arm a tug and pulled him into a hug while giving his hair a gentle tousle. A hug. He couldn't remember the last time anyone had hugged him. He had always just felt like the problem child that they people obligated to take on. But this, this felt so good and so strange. Feeling his hard, protective shell of an exterior beginning to soften, he quickly pulled back, and gave the man a nod.

The days turned into weeks. He couldn't understand this strange family. They were kind to each other, and, they all seemed genuinely happy. He tried to keep to himself. He stayed very quiet - observing them. He had been betrayed and rejected enough. He wasn't about to let that happen again. He opted out of family games and movies nights - observing from a distance. As the time went by, he found that even though he still refused to vocalize any thoughts out loud, every now and then he would laugh. He would actually laugh. It was such a foreign sound coming out of his mouth that it would shock him back into silence. He couldn't remember laughing before now. Not ever.

He found himself wanting it all to be real - forever. Yet, deep inside, the fear that he was going to mess up and ruin everything again kept nagging at him. What he didn't know was that his life was about to change forever. He had agreed to go to a church youth service with his older foster brother, Adam. Adam was 15 years old, which was just two years older than he was. Adam had told him how he had spent several years in foster care before coming to stay with this family where he was eventually adopted. Adam seemed happy, content even. Could he ever feel that way as well?

That night at the youth service the boy tried to listen to the speaker. The speaker kept talking about God and how he was a good father. The boy struggled to grasp that kind of father. Although, his foster dad did seem pretty cool. Maybe God was kind of like that?

The more the speaker spoke, the more uncomfortable the boy became. What was this he was feeling? As the speaker spoke of God's love, a lump formed in his throat and tears filled his eyes. *"No! No! Don't let them see you cry!" h*e screamed in his mind. Yet, he was undone in what felt like a warm pool of pure love and total acceptance. The pull on his heart was near agonizing as it started to break the solid fortress of protection around his heart. The pain within him was now coming face to face with that love - that pure and total love. Standing to his feet he made his way to the front of the room to where the preacher was speaking - the boy was oblivious to the other youth in the room or the fact that he preacher hadn't called anyone forward. He stood there, in the front of the room facing the preacher, tears streaming down his face and said, *"I want God to be my father. I want this love I feel now - forever."*

The preacher's eyes filled with tears of his own as he reached out and hugged the boy. Then smiling through his tears the preacher led him in a prayer.

"Dear Father in Heaven, thank you for loving me. Thank-you that you loved me so much that you gave your only son to die in my place. I receive your love for me. Thank-you for being my Father."

In that moment, he felt as though every heavy thing was lifted off his shoulders. His pain was being washed away through his tears. All of the hardness in him was melting away in this love he was feeling - this perfect and complete love. He knew now that he would never again be alone - that his Father would always be with him - forever.

"The Lord is close to all whose hearts are crushed by pain, and he is always ready to restore the repentant one."

Psalms 34:18 TPT

"The light of God's love shined within us when he sent his matchless Son into the world so that we might live through him. This is love: He loved us long before we loved him. It was his love, not ours. He proved it by sending his Son to be the pleasing sacrificial offering to take away our sins."

1 John 4:9-10 TPT

Have you ever struggled with longing to belong? Perhaps like the young man in this story, you too have been without a family to call your own. Or perhaps, the family you had rejected or abandoned you. We were created for family and connection. It was God's design that you should be in a family. Sadly, for many, the family is the place of fear and wounding rather than that safe place full of love and acceptance. If you have ever struggled with feeling abandoned and rejected - if you have been longing to belong, God wants you to know and experience his love right now. God, the Father made a way for us to become part of his family. If you're wanting to experience His love for you and become His child, pray this prayer with me.

"God, thank-you that I can be part of your family. Thank-you that I can call you my Father. I accept the sacrifice that your son made for me, so that I can experience your love. Thank-you that you promise to stay close to the broken-hearted. Help me now to rest in your love. I pray this now in Jesus' name. Amen."

The Ultimate Sacrifice

"BANG! BANG! BANG! BANG!"

The loud banging on the door brought him to his feet. He could hear the crowd outside yelling and chanting. Walking towards the door the sounds of their chanting became more clear and the door shook with every hit as if it were being slammed by a battering ram. Upon reaching the door, he placed one hand on the rattling handle and hung his head to pray. "Father, not my will, but yours be done here tonight." He paused and the noise of the crowds became a distant din.

In that moment, the nearness of his Father gave him strength. Taking a deep breath, he raised his head and turned the handle. The door flew open as the crowd simultaneously charged the door knocking him backwards. Hands reached out and grabbed at his clothes and his arms, dragging him forward onto the front step to face the mob.

Looking out he could see his friends and those he had helped only earlier that week, sharing truth, hope and love with them. As he looked into their faces they all one-by-one turned their eyes from his and tried to melt into the crowd as if to blend in. The pain stabbed his heart. He loved these people so. Yet, they were so lost. Suddenly, he was alone. Only the faces of those who were intent on silencing him could be seen. Yet, he drew strength from his Father. His Father had always been with him - always. Even now as he turned his gaze away from the crowd he saw his Father looking towards him.

Without warning, a blow was struck to his back and he fell forward down the porch steps. The crowd encircled him as he stumbled, dragging and pushing him into the street. There, they began to carry out such heinous and hateful acts of brutality, intent on taking his life. His only crime - they didn't like what he had to say. They didn't want to hear it. Blow after blow was dealt. Opening his eyes, face down in the asphalt, the smell of the street and dust filled his nose as blood and tears flowing over his eyes blurred the flurry of boots flying towards his body with incredible force.

But one face he could still see. It's him, his father. Struggling to lift his head to see his father's face more clearly he saw his father's tear drenched cheeks as he cried for his child - his only son. *"I just need to look into his eyes,"* he thought. Trying to focus and lift his gaze, his body being pummelled and bludgeoned by the mob, he struggled to lift himself onto his knees. Finally, his gaze reached the eyes of his father. In that moment, his father raised both of his hands and hid his face, turning his back on the horrible scene of grotesque pain and vile hatred before him. He watched his Father's back as he walked away, slumped over with his face in his hands weeping.

Suddenly, a loneliness more painful than the wounds being inflicted upon his body cut deep into his soul and he let out a wretched and anguished scream, "DAD!" "DADDY!" "Why did you leave me?" Then, in pain and a loneliness deeper, darker and more painful than is humanly possible to bare, his head fell to the pavement, and he took his final breath.

This man's name is Jesus. He experienced the ultimate loneliness so that you and I would never have to. That ultimate loneliness was separation from God. Even in your darkest hour, you can call on Him, and he'll answer. He is always there for you. When Jesus was being killed - killed to pay the price for our sins and failures - his Father, God, had to turn away from him. In Jesus' darkest hour, his Father left him alone. This had to happen. You see, Jesus at that time, was carrying all of the filth and shame for all of mankind. He bore it upon himself on the cross, so that you would be free from that debt. God, his Father, could not look upon sin, so had to turn his back in that moment. If you think that that moment wasn't horrible and excruciating for Jesus, you're mistaken. It was horrific. It was the darkest and deepest loneliness that ever could be and ever was experienced.

Now, because Jesus paid the penalty for all of your failures, you have free and open access to God, the Father. There will never be a situation in your life that is so dark and so horrible that he cannot be with you. All you need to do is ask him to be there with you. Call out to him. He's eagerly waiting to be invited into your situation. He wants to walk with you through every sorrow and every joy. You may not understand the type of love he has for you, but he wants to show you everyday, for the rest of your life, just how full and complete his love for you is.

So now, as you think and meditate on God's love for you, I pray for a greater release of God's grace, love, and total well-being to flow into your life from God our Father and from our Lord Jesus Christ! May God give you a greater understanding of His great love towards you - right now in this very moment. May you experience the gracious love of God reaching into the deepest darkest parts of you and making you whole.

"He Was Despised and Rejected by Men,
a Man of Deep Sorrows
Who Was no Stranger to
Suffering and Grief.
We Hid our Faces From Him in Disgust
and Considered Him a Nobody,
Not Worthy of Respect.
Yet He Was the One
Who Carried our Sicknesses
and Endured the Torment
Of our Sufferings.
We Viewed Him as One

Who Was Being Punished
for Something He Himself Had Done,
as One Who Was Struck Down by God
And Brought Low.
But It Was Because of our Rebellious Deeds
That He Was Pierced
and Because of our Sins
That He Was Crushed.
He Endured the Punishment
That Made Us Completely Whole,
and in his Wounding
We Found our Healing.
Like Wayward Sheep,
We Have all Wandered Astray.
Each of Us Has Turned From God's Paths
And Chosen our Own Way;
Even So, Yahweh Laid the Guilt of our Every
Sin Upon Him.
He Was Oppressed and Harshly Mistreated;
Still He Humbly Submitted,

Refusing To Defend Himself.
He Was Brought Like a Gentle Lamb
To Be Slaughtered.
Like a Silent Sheep Before his Shearers,
He Didn't Even Open his Mouth.
By Coercion And
With a Perversion of Justice
He Was Taken Away.
And Who Could Have
Imagined his Future?
He Was Cut Down in the Prime of Life;
for the Rebellion of his Own People,
He Was Struck Down in Their Place.
They Gave Him a Grave Among Criminals,
but He Ended Up Instead
In a Rich Man's Tomb,
Although He Had Done no Violence nor
Spoken Deceitfully.

Isaiah 53:2-9 TPT

"Father, I thank you that you gave your son to pay the price for all of my sins. Thank-you that because of Jesus' sacrifice, I am able to come to you without hindrance. Thank-you, Jesus, for bearing the pain of ultimate loneliness and the weight of my sin and shame, when you suffered and died for me. You, O Lord, are good, and your mercy and love are everlasting. I praise you and thank you for your immeasurable love for me. Amen"

ABOUT THE AUTHOR

A professional life coach and author, Pamela resides in northern Alberta, Canada with her husband and four children. Pamela has walked through the loneliness of abusive relationships, divorce and single parenting and calls her life *"a testimony of God's grace and faithfulness"*. Now, Pamela commits her time to raising her family along side her husband, and sharing the hope and love that she's found, through her writing and life coaching. Pamela has a passion to not only help people find wholeness for their souls, but also for their bodies. In her book *"Living Well - developing habits for healthy living"* , Pamela shares part of her passion to see others find freedom from sickness by learning new lifestyle habits. As you read through this book, it is Pamela's prayer that you meet God and His love for you as your Father and faithful friend, and that you experience healing in your soul.

Manufactured by Amazon.ca
Bolton, ON